North Korea's Illicit Businesses Supporting the Communist Dictatorship

AF424176

Copyright Page

TITLE: North Korea's Illicit Businesses Supporting the Communist Dictatorship

1ST Edition

Copyright @ 2023

Roberto M. Rodriguez. All rights reserved.

ISBN: 9798223511229

Table of Contents

North Korea's Illicit Businesses Supporting the Communist Dictatorship

By Roberto Miguel Rodriguez

Chapter 1: Introduction to North Korea's Shadow Economy

Understanding the Shadow Economy

The shadow economy refers to a clandestine network of illicit businesses that operate outside the boundaries of legal frameworks and regulations. In the case of North Korea, the shadow economy plays a pivotal role in supporting the communist dictatorship, ensuring its survival and financing its activities. This subchapter aims to shed light on various facets of the shadow economy in North Korea, providing a comprehensive understanding of the illegal businesses that enable the regime to maintain its grip on power.

Arms smuggling is a prominent aspect of the shadow economy, as the North Korean regime relies on the illegal trade of weapons to strengthen its military capabilities and suppress any potential threats. This subchapter will delve into the mechanisms involved in the smuggling of arms and explore how it sustains the communist dictatorship.

Another critical source of income for the regime is counterfeit currency production. By printing fake money, the North Korean government can fund its operations and maintain control over the economy. This subchapter will examine the techniques employed in counterfeit currency production and its implications for the regime's financial stability.

Drug trafficking also plays a significant role in generating income for the regime. The illegal smuggling and sale of drugs provide a lucrative source of revenue while fueling addiction and social instability. This subchapter will explore the extent of North Korea's involvement in drug trafficking and its impact on both domestic and international communities.

Furthermore, the shadow economy in North Korea encompasses human trafficking, cybercrime, nuclear proliferation, wildlife smuggling, money laundering, illegal fishing, and illicit trade in natural resources. Each of these activities serves as a financial lifeline for the communist dictatorship, enabling it to sustain its oppressive regime.

By understanding the intricacies of the shadow economy in North Korea, diplomats can gain valuable insights into the inner workings of the regime. This knowledge will not only aid in formulating effective policies to combat these illicit businesses but also contribute to efforts aimed at promoting human rights, regional stability, and denuclearization on the Korean Peninsula.

In conclusion, the shadow economy in North Korea encompasses a wide array of illegal businesses that provide essential funding for the communist dictatorship. Arms smuggling, counterfeit currency production, drug trafficking, human trafficking, cybercrime, nuclear proliferation, wildlife smuggling, money laundering, illegal fishing, and illicit trade in natural resources all contribute to the regime's survival. By comprehending the intricacies of the shadow economy, diplomats can work towards dismantling these illicit networks and promoting a more prosperous and stable North Korea.

The Significance of North Korea's Illicit Businesses

North Korea's illicit businesses play a crucial role in supporting the communist dictatorship, and it is imperative for diplomats and global stakeholders to understand their significance. This subchapter aims to shed light on the various illegal activities that sustain the regime economically, enabling it to maintain its grip on power.

One of the primary sources of income for the North Korean regime is arms smuggling. Through illegal trade of weapons, the regime garners significant funds, which are then channeled towards its military ambitions and the suppression of its own people. This illicit trade not only poses a threat to regional stability but also enables North Korea to sustain its oppressive regime.

Counterfeit currency production is another illicit business that the regime heavily relies on. By printing fake money, North Korea funds its communist dictatorship and circumvents international sanctions. This illegal activity undermines global financial systems and poses a significant challenge to the international community.

Drug trafficking is yet another lucrative venture for the North Korean regime. Smuggling and selling illegal drugs generate substantial income, which is then used to fuel the regime's activities. This not only contributes to the global drug trade but also perpetuates addiction and suffering among the North Korean people.

Human trafficking is a grave violation of human rights that the regime exploits to finance its communist dictatorship. The illegal trade of humans for forced labor or exploitation enables the regime to profit while subjecting individuals to unimaginable suffering.

In recent years, North Korea has expanded its involvement in cybercrime, engaging in hacking, phishing, and other cyber activities for financial gain. These illicit activities not only pose a threat to global cybersecurity but also provide the regime with additional revenue streams.

Moreover, North Korea's illicit businesses extend to nuclear proliferation, wildlife smuggling, money laundering, illegal fishing, and illicit trade in natural resources. These activities enable the regime to sustain its nuclear program, exploit endangered species and natural resources, and generate income through illegal means.

Understanding the significance of North Korea's illicit businesses is essential for diplomats and global stakeholders. By comprehending the various illegal activities that support the communist dictatorship, effective strategies can be developed to counter and dismantle these illicit networks. Diplomatic efforts, along with international cooperation and sanctions, are crucial in curbing North Korea's illicit businesses and bringing about a more stable and prosperous future for the North Korean people.

The Impact on the Communist Dictatorship

The shadow economy in North Korea plays a crucial role in supporting the communist dictatorship, and its impact on the regime cannot be underestimated. In this subchapter, we will explore the various illegal businesses that sustain the North Korean government, shedding light on the consequences of these activities.

One of the primary sources of income for the regime is arms smuggling. North Korea engages in the illegal trade of weapons, providing arms to other rogue states and militant groups. This not only funds the communist dictatorship but also destabilizes regions and threatens global security.

Counterfeit currency production is another illicit business that significantly impacts the communist dictatorship. The regime prints fake money, circulating it worldwide to generate funds. This undermines the economic stability of nations and erodes trust in financial systems.

Drug trafficking is yet another lucrative source of income for the regime. North Korea smuggles and sells illegal drugs, such as methamphetamine, to generate substantial revenue. This illicit activity not only fuels addiction and harms societies but also enables the communist dictatorship to finance its oppressive regime.

Human trafficking is a despicable practice employed by the regime to finance its operations. The illegal trade of humans for forced labor or exploitation provides a steady flow of income for the communist dictatorship. This heinous activity results in the suffering and enslavement of countless individuals.

The involvement of North Korea in cybercrime is another means to generate funds for the regime. Hacking, phishing, and other cyber activities enable the communist dictatorship to engage in financial fraud and theft, impacting individuals, businesses, and governments worldwide.

Nuclear proliferation is a grave concern associated with the communist dictatorship. North Korea's illegal sale of nuclear materials or technology supports its nuclear program, posing a significant threat to global peace and security.

Wildlife smuggling is another illicit business that directly impacts the communist dictatorship. The illegal trade of endangered species and animal products generates substantial revenue for the regime while contributing to the destruction of biodiversity.

Money laundering is a critical component of the shadow economy, as it enables illicit funds to appear legitimate. The regime employs various illegal means to make their revenue streams undetectable, further sustaining the communist dictatorship.

Illegal fishing and illicit trade in natural resources also play a significant role in supporting the regime. North Korea engages in unregulated and illegal fishing activities to generate income, depleting marine resources and threatening ecosystems. Additionally, the smuggling of minerals, timber, and other natural resources further funds the communist dictatorship while exploiting the country's resources for personal gain.

In conclusion, the impact of the shadow economy on the communist dictatorship in North Korea is far-reaching and destructive. The various illicit businesses, including arms smuggling, counterfeit currency production, drug trafficking, human trafficking, cybercrime, nuclear proliferation, wildlife smuggling, money laundering, illegal fishing, and illicit trade in natural resources, not only maintain the oppressive regime but also pose significant threats to global security, stability, and the well-being of individuals worldwide. It is imperative for diplomats and international communities to understand and address these issues to undermine the communist dictatorship and promote a more just and sustainable future.

The Purpose of this Book

Welcome, esteemed diplomats, to "The Shadow Economy: Unveiling North Korea's Illicit Businesses Supporting the Communist Dictatorship." This subchapter aims to provide you with a comprehensive understanding of the purpose and significance of this book, catering specifically to your interests in North Korea's illegal businesses to support the communist dictatorship.

The primary objective of this book is to shed light on the clandestine activities that have been fueling the North Korean regime's oppressive rule. By delving into the various branches of the shadow economy that sustain the communist dictatorship, we seek to expose the inner workings of a regime that thrives on illicit practices.

Through meticulous research and extensive analysis, we have identified several key areas of illicit businesses that are central to supporting the North Korean regime. These include arms smuggling, counterfeit currency production, drug trafficking, human trafficking, cybercrime, nuclear proliferation, wildlife smuggling, money laundering, illegal fishing, and illicit trade in natural resources. Each of these niches plays a critical role in financing the communist dictatorship, ensuring its survival against international pressures and sanctions.

By exploring these topics, we aim to equip diplomats like you with an in-depth understanding of the mechanisms employed by the North

Korean regime to sustain itself. This knowledge will empower you to make informed decisions and develop effective strategies to counter these illicit activities. Furthermore, understanding the shadow economy will enable you to grasp the complexity of North Korea's economic landscape and its implications for regional and global security.

As you delve into the chapters of this book, you will encounter detailed accounts, expert analyses, and revealing insights into each aspect of North Korea's illegal businesses. We have gathered information from intelligence reports, testimonies, and extensive research to paint a comprehensive picture of the shadow economy.

We hope that this book serves as a valuable resource for diplomats like you, allowing you to better comprehend the multifaceted challenges posed by the North Korean regime's illicit activities. By uncovering the hidden layers of the shadow economy, we strive to contribute to the collective effort in combating these illegal practices and promoting a more secure and stable world.

Thank you for your dedication to diplomacy, and we trust that "The Shadow Economy: Unveiling North Korea's Illicit Businesses Supporting the Communist Dictatorship" will be an enlightening and thought-provoking read for you.

Chapter 2: North Korea's Illegal Businesses to Support the Communist Dictatorship

Overview of North Korea's Shadow Economy

The shadow economy of North Korea plays a crucial role in sustaining the communist dictatorship that governs the nation. This subchapter aims to provide diplomats and other interested parties with an in-depth understanding of the various illicit businesses that operate within the country to support the regime.

One of the primary sources of income for the North Korean regime is arms smuggling. The illegal trade of weapons provides the regime with the necessary resources to maintain a strong military presence and suppress any internal threats to their power.

Another significant aspect of the shadow economy is counterfeit currency production. The regime engages in the printing of fake money, which they circulate both domestically and internationally to fund their activities. This practice allows them to maintain a steady flow of funds while bypassing international sanctions.

Drug trafficking is another major source of income for the communist dictatorship. North Korea is involved in smuggling and selling illegal drugs, such as methamphetamine and heroin, to generate substantial profits. These funds are utilized to finance various aspects of the regime, including their nuclear program.

Human trafficking is also prevalent in North Korea, with the regime engaging in the illegal trade of humans for forced labor or exploitation. This abhorrent practice not only generates income for the communist dictatorship but also serves as a means of controlling the population and maintaining their grip on power.

Cybercrime has emerged as a significant threat, with North Korea actively engaging in hacking, phishing, and other cyber activities for financial gain. These illicit activities allow the regime to acquire funds while also furthering their technological capabilities.

Nuclear proliferation is another concerning aspect of North Korea's shadow economy. The regime is involved in the illegal sale of nuclear materials or technology, which aids in the development and expansion of their nuclear program, posing a significant threat to regional and global security.

The illicit trade in wildlife and animal products is also rampant in North Korea. The regime profits from the illegal trade of endangered species, exploiting the natural resources within the country for financial gain.

Money laundering is a prevalent practice within the shadow economy. The regime employs various illegal means to make their illicit funds appear legitimate, allowing them to continue their operations despite international sanctions.

Illegal fishing and the illicit trade in natural resources further contribute to the regime's income. North Korea engages in unregulated and illegal fishing activities, depleting marine resources and generating substantial profits. Additionally, the smuggling of minerals, timber, and other natural resources provides further financial support to the communist dictatorship.

This subchapter serves as an eye-opening overview of the extensive illicit businesses that underpin North Korea's shadow economy. Understanding the various dimensions of this economy is crucial for diplomats and stakeholders seeking to address the ongoing challenges posed by the communist regime and its illegal activities.

The Role of Illegal Businesses in Sustaining the Regime

Title: The Role of Illegal Businesses in Sustaining the Regime

Introduction:

In the clandestine world of North Korea, a shadow economy thrives, supporting the communist dictatorship and undermining international efforts to bring about change. This subchapter explores the various illicit businesses that sustain the regime, enabling it to maintain power and control over its citizens. From arms smuggling to counterfeit currency production, drug trafficking to human trafficking, the regime employs a range of illegal activities to generate income. This chapter aims to shed light on the intricate web of North Korea's illicit businesses and their impact on the country and its people.

Arms Smuggling:

One of the primary ways the regime sustains itself is through the illegal trade of weapons. By supplying arms to other rogue states and non-state actors, North Korea generates significant revenue while strengthening its position in the global arena. Arms smuggling not only bolsters the regime's military capabilities but also fosters instability in regions where conflicts persist.

Counterfeit Currency Production:

To fund its communist dictatorship, North Korea engages in the production of counterfeit currencies. This sophisticated operation allows the regime to inject illicit funds into the global financial system, rendering its activities harder to trace. By undermining the integrity of international economies, North Korea further strengthens its grip on power.

Drug Trafficking:

The illegal trade of drugs has become a lucrative business for the regime, providing substantial income streams. North Korea's involvement in drug trafficking ranges from cultivating and smuggling methamphetamines to producing and distributing other narcotics. This trade not only generates revenue but also contributes to the destabilization of societies and undermines global efforts to combat drug abuse.

Human Trafficking:

North Korea's communist dictatorship goes to extreme lengths to finance its operations, including the illegal trade of humans for forced labor and exploitation. Human trafficking not only generates income but also serves as a means of controlling its citizens. This illicit practice not only violates human rights but perpetuates a cycle of abuse and oppression.

Cybercrime:

North Korea's involvement in cybercrime has gained international attention. The regime engages in hacking, phishing, and other cyber activities to gain financial resources and further its political agenda. By targeting financial institutions, businesses, and governments, they exploit vulnerabilities in cyberspace, posing a significant threat to global security.

Conclusion:

The role of illegal businesses in sustaining the North Korean regime is not only a concern for the international community but also a violation of human rights and a threat to global stability. Arms smuggling, counterfeit currency production, drug trafficking, human trafficking, cybercrime, nuclear proliferation, wildlife smuggling, money laundering, illegal fishing, and illicit trade in natural resources are all integral to the survival of the communist dictatorship. As diplomats, it is crucial to understand and address these illicit activities to bring about meaningful change and promote a better future for North Korea and its people.

The Challenges of Investigating Illicit Activities in North Korea

Introduction:

In the isolated nation of North Korea, the communist dictatorship thrives on a shadow economy sustained by a range of illicit activities. These activities, designed to generate income for the regime, pose significant challenges for investigators attempting to uncover the truth behind North Korea's illegal businesses. This subchapter delves into the various challenges faced by diplomats while investigating illicit activities in North Korea, shedding light on the complex web of illegal enterprises that support the communist dictatorship.

Understanding the Shadow Economy:

North Korea's illegal businesses serve as a lifeline for the regime, enabling it to flout international sanctions and maintain its oppressive hold on power. From arms smuggling and counterfeit currency production to drug trafficking and human trafficking, the regime engages in a wide array of illicit activities to fund its operations. Investigating these ventures requires diplomats to navigate a web of secrecy, corruption, and state-controlled information.

Secrecy and Lack of Cooperation:

One of the foremost challenges in investigating illicit activities in North Korea is the regime's culture of secrecy. The communist dictatorship goes to great lengths to conceal its illegal enterprises, making it difficult for investigators to gather concrete evidence. Additionally, the lack of cooperation from North Korean authorities further complicates the task, as they are unwilling to disclose any information that may expose their illicit operations.

Corruption and Bribery:

Corruption permeates every aspect of North Korean society, making it challenging for diplomats to gather reliable information. High-ranking officials often turn a blind eye to illicit activities in exchange for bribes, further hindering investigations. This culture of corruption creates an environment where the truth is difficult to ascertain, and investigators must be cautious in their dealings to avoid being misled or compromised.

Limited Access and Surveillance:

North Korea tightly controls access to the country, making it challenging for diplomats to conduct on-the-ground investigations. The regime heavily surveils its citizens and restricts foreign involvement, making it difficult to gather firsthand accounts or corroborate information. Diplomats face constant surveillance and scrutiny, limiting their ability to gather evidence or build networks of informants.

Conclusion:

Investigating the illicit activities that sustain North Korea's communist dictatorship is a daunting task for diplomats. The regime's secrecy, lack of cooperation, corruption, limited access, and surveillance present significant challenges that impede efforts to uncover the truth. However, despite these obstacles, diplomats must persist in their pursuit of justice and accountability, working together to shed light on the shadow economy that supports the oppressive regime. Only through continued diligence and international cooperation can we hope to dismantle the illicit businesses that enable the communist dictatorship to maintain its grip on power.

Chapter 3: Arms Smuggling: Illegal Trade of Weapons to Support the North Korean Regime

The Arms Trade Landscape in North Korea

The illicit arms trade plays a crucial role in supporting the North Korean regime, enabling it to maintain its iron grip on power and pursue its aggressive agenda. This subchapter will delve into the intricate web of illegal arms smuggling that sustains the communist dictatorship, shedding light on the various actors involved and the devastating consequences for regional and global security.

North Korea's arms smuggling activities are widespread and sophisticated, involving a network of state-sponsored entities, intermediaries, and criminal organizations. The regime leverages these networks to acquire and distribute a wide range of conventional weapons, including small arms, ballistic missiles, and even nuclear technology. This not only fuels regional tensions but also poses a grave threat to international peace and stability.

One of the primary motivations behind the North Korean regime's arms trade is financial gain. The illegal sale of weapons generates substantial revenue for the communist dictatorship, allowing it to fund its military apparatus and divert resources away from the impoverished population. Diplomats and policymakers must be aware of these financial incentives as they seek to dismantle the illicit arms networks that sustain the regime.

Furthermore, the arms trade is closely intertwined with other illegal businesses that support the North Korean regime. Counterfeit currency production, drug trafficking, human trafficking, cybercrime, nuclear proliferation, wildlife smuggling, money laundering, illegal fishing, and illicit trade in natural resources all contribute to the regime's financial lifeline. Understanding the interconnected nature of these illicit activities is crucial for developing effective strategies to disrupt and dismantle the shadow economy that sustains the communist dictatorship.

By shedding light on the arms trade landscape in North Korea, this subchapter aims to equip diplomats with the knowledge and insights necessary to counter the regime's illicit activities. It underscores the urgency of international cooperation and robust countermeasures to curb the flow of weapons, disrupt financial networks, and hold accountable those who enable the North Korean regime's dangerous ambitions.

Only by understanding the multifaceted nature of North Korea's illicit businesses can the international community effectively tackle the root causes of the communist dictatorship's resilience. Diplomats and policymakers must work together to disrupt this shadow economy and foster conditions for a more peaceful, prosperous future on the Korean Peninsula and beyond.

The Role of Arms Smuggling in Financing the Regime

Arms smuggling plays a crucial role in financing the North Korean regime, supporting its communist dictatorship and allowing it to maintain its oppressive grip on power. This subchapter aims to shed light on the illicit businesses that sustain the regime, with a specific focus on the illegal trade of weapons.

The North Korean regime, led by Kim Jong-un, relies heavily on arms smuggling to generate income and acquire the necessary resources to maintain its military capabilities. Diplomats need to be aware of this illicit trade to better understand the regime's activities and devise effective strategies to counter them.

Arms smuggling involves the illegal trade of weapons, including firearms, ammunition, and even advanced military technology, to support the North Korean regime. These weapons are often acquired through illicit channels and sold to various groups and nations that have no qualms about violating international arms embargoes.

The profits generated from arms smuggling are then funneled back into the regime, allowing it to sustain its military infrastructure, develop and enhance its nuclear program, and suppress dissent within its borders. This subchapter explores the intricate networks that facilitate this trade, highlighting the complicity of both state and non-state actors in perpetuating the cycle of violence and oppression.

Understanding the role of arms smuggling in financing the regime is crucial for diplomats, as it provides insight into the North Korean regime's priorities and motivations. By comprehending the regime's reliance on illicit weapons trade, diplomats can work towards cutting off this vital source of income and disrupting the regime's ability to carry out its nefarious activities.

In the following chapters, we will delve into other illicit businesses that support the communist dictatorship, including counterfeit currency production, drug trafficking, human trafficking, cybercrime, nuclear proliferation, wildlife smuggling, money laundering, illegal fishing, and illicit trade in natural resources. By exploring these interconnected facets of the shadow economy, we will gain a comprehensive understanding of the North Korean regime's illicit activities and the challenges they pose to international security and stability.

Overall, this subchapter serves as an introduction to the role of arms smuggling in financing the North Korean regime and sets the stage for a deeper exploration of the various illicit businesses that sustain the communist dictatorship. Diplomats must be well-informed about these issues to effectively address the challenges posed by North Korea's illegal activities and work towards a more peaceful and secure future.

International Efforts to Combat Arms Smuggling in North Korea

Introduction:

The illicit activities conducted by the North Korean regime have been a cause of concern for the international community. One such activity, arms smuggling, poses a significant threat to regional and global security. This subchapter will highlight the international efforts to combat arms smuggling in North Korea and the impact of these efforts on the communist dictatorship.

Background:

North Korea's illegal arms trade has been a key source of revenue for the regime, enabling it to strengthen its military capabilities and further its aggressive agenda. The regime's involvement in arms smuggling not only destabilizes the region but also poses a grave threat to international peace and security.

International Efforts:

1. United Nations Security Council Resolutions:

The United Nations Security Council (UNSC) has adopted numerous resolutions imposing sanctions on North Korea, specifically targeting its arms smuggling activities. These resolutions aim to restrict the regime's access to conventional weapons and related technologies. They also call upon member states to intercept and seize any shipments of arms destined for or originating from North Korea.

2. Enhanced Maritime Interdiction:

Coordinated efforts by international naval forces have been instrumental in combating arms smuggling in North Korea. Through increased surveillance and interdiction operations, these forces have intercepted and seized numerous illicit shipments of weapons. This has significantly disrupted the regime's ability to acquire arms and has dealt a blow to its military capabilities.

3. Strengthening Financial Controls:

Efforts to combat arms smuggling in North Korea also involve targeting the financial networks that facilitate these illicit activities. By implementing stringent financial controls and sanctions, the international community aims to cut off the regime's access to funds generated through arms smuggling, making it increasingly difficult for the regime to sustain its military ambitions.

4. International Cooperation:

International cooperation plays a crucial role in combating arms smuggling in North Korea. Countries have been sharing intelligence, exchanging information, and cooperating in joint operations to intercept and seize illicit arms shipments. Additionally, diplomatic efforts have been made to garner support for the enforcement of sanctions and ensure compliance from all member states.

Impact on the Communist Dictatorship:

These international efforts to combat arms smuggling have had a significant impact on the North Korean regime. By disrupting the flow of weapons, the international community has limited the regime's ability to enhance its military capabilities. This has not only diminished the regime's threat to regional security but has also weakened its position in international negotiations, making it more amenable to diplomatic solutions.

Conclusion:

International efforts to combat arms smuggling in North Korea have been crucial in curbing the regime's ability to acquire and proliferate weapons. By implementing sanctions, enhancing maritime interdiction, strengthening financial controls, and fostering international cooperation, the international community has demonstrated its resolve to confront illicit activities supporting the communist dictatorship. These efforts have not only contributed to regional stability but have also nudged the regime towards engaging in diplomatic negotiations and seeking peaceful resolutions to the ongoing tensions. However, continued vigilance and robust enforcement of these measures are necessary to deprive the regime of the resources it needs to sustain its aggressive agenda.

Chapter 4: Counterfeit Currency Production: Printing Fake Money to Fund the Communist Dictatorship

The Counterfeit Currency Network in North Korea

North Korea's illicit activities have long been a concern for the international community, with the communist dictatorship relying on various illegal businesses to support its regime. One of the most prominent among these is the counterfeit currency network, a clandestine operation responsible for printing fake money to fund the regime's activities.

Counterfeit currency production has become a lucrative venture for the North Korean government, providing them with an alternative source of income that is difficult to trace. Diplomats and experts have been closely monitoring this illegal trade, as it not only undermines the stability of global financial systems but also poses a threat to national security.

The counterfeit currency network operates through a sophisticated web of agents and intermediaries, spanning across different countries. North Korean operatives, well-trained in the art of counterfeiting, produce high-quality counterfeit bills, including US dollars, euros, and Chinese yuan. These fake currencies are then distributed through various channels, often through illicit networks involved in money laundering and smuggling.

The North Korean regime's involvement in counterfeit currency production is not a new phenomenon. Over the years, they have mastered the art of deception, constantly adapting their techniques to evade detection. Advanced printing technologies, such as intaglio printing and microprinting, are employed to create counterfeit bills that are almost indistinguishable from genuine currency.

The profits derived from counterfeit currency production are used to support the regime's nefarious activities, including its nuclear program, arms smuggling, and human trafficking. These ill-gotten funds contribute to the consolidation of power by the communist dictatorship, enabling them to suppress dissent and maintain control over the population.

Addressing the issue of the counterfeit currency network in North Korea requires a concerted effort from the international community. Diplomats must collaborate to strengthen financial regulations, enhance intelligence sharing, and improve coordination to disrupt these illicit networks. Additionally, targeted sanctions and diplomatic pressure should be applied to countries that facilitate or turn a blind eye to this illegal trade.

By unveiling the extent of North Korea's involvement in counterfeit currency production, diplomats can expose the true nature of the regime and garner support for robust measures to dismantle this illicit network. Only through a united front can we hope to curb the flow of counterfeit currency and deprive the North Korean regime of the funds it needs to sustain its communist dictatorship.

Techniques and Methods Used in Counterfeit Currency Production

Counterfeit currency production is a prevalent and illicit practice employed by the North Korean regime to generate funds for the communist dictatorship. This subchapter aims to shed light on the various techniques and methods utilized in this illegal trade, providing an in-depth understanding of the mechanics behind counterfeit currency production.

The first technique employed by the regime involves the acquisition of genuine banknotes from foreign countries. Diplomats must be aware that North Korea has established an extensive network of agents and operatives who procure authentic currencies, primarily from neighboring countries. These banknotes serve as templates for the production of counterfeit bills.

The production process begins with the meticulous reproduction of physical security features present in genuine banknotes. Sophisticated printing techniques, such as offset printing or intaglio printing, are employed to replicate intricate design elements, watermarks, and holographic features. Diplomats must understand that the regime's counterfeit operations have significantly evolved over the years, resulting in counterfeit bills that closely resemble genuine currency.

To further enhance the authenticity of counterfeit banknotes, the regime employs chemical treatments. These treatments help replicate the distinct texture, feel, and durability of genuine currency. Diplomats should note that North Korea has access to advanced equipment, including high-quality printing presses and specialized ink formulations, enabling them to produce counterfeit bills of exceptional quality.

Furthermore, the regime employs skilled artisans who meticulously handcraft the intricate details present in genuine banknotes. These skilled craftsmen utilize a range of tools, including micro-engraving needles and magnification devices, to reproduce minute details, such as fine lines and microprints.

It is crucial for diplomats to be aware that the North Korean regime constantly adapts its counterfeit currency production techniques to outsmart law enforcement agencies and financial institutions. They frequently alter their printing methods, security features, and even target different currencies to evade detection.

In conclusion, this subchapter provides diplomats with a comprehensive insight into the techniques and methods employed by the North Korean regime in counterfeit currency production. Understanding these clandestine practices is essential in combating this illicit trade and curbing the financial resources that support the communist dictatorship.

The Economic and Political Implications of Counterfeit Currency

Counterfeit currency production is one of the key illicit businesses that support the communist dictatorship in North Korea. This subchapter delves into the economic and political implications of this activity, shedding light on the far-reaching consequences it has for both the country itself and the international community.

From an economic standpoint, the production of counterfeit currency serves as a critical revenue stream for the North Korean regime. By printing fake money, they can fund their various operations and maintain their grip on power. The influx of counterfeit bills into circulation not only destabilizes the domestic economy but also undermines the value of legitimate currencies in the global market. This devaluation can lead to economic instability, affecting trade and investment worldwide.

On the political front, the implications of counterfeit currency are equally significant. The production and distribution of fake money are intricately linked to the regime's survival. The North Korean government uses these illicit funds to finance its military apparatus, support its nuclear program, and sustain its oppressive policies. By understanding the impact of counterfeit currency, diplomats can gain insight into the inner workings of the communist dictatorship and take appropriate measures to counter its influence.

Moreover, the use of counterfeit currency has broader international security implications. The regime's involvement in counterfeiting operations demonstrates its willingness to engage in illegal activities to achieve its goals. This raises concerns about the country's overall commitment to international norms and its potential involvement in other illicit endeavors, such as arms smuggling, drug trafficking, or cybercrime. As diplomats, it is crucial to recognize the interconnected nature of these illegal businesses and the need for a comprehensive approach to tackle the challenges posed by the North Korean regime.

Addressing the economic and political implications of counterfeit currency production requires a multi-faceted response. It involves strengthening domestic and international efforts to combat money laundering, enhancing border security measures, and promoting financial transparency. Additionally, diplomatic engagement, sanctions, and cooperation with international organizations are pivotal in curbing the North Korean regime's illicit activities.

By understanding the economic and political implications of counterfeit currency production, diplomats can play a vital role in dismantling the shadow economy that supports the communist dictatorship in North Korea. Through concerted efforts, the international community can work towards promoting stability, human rights, and global security.

Chapter 5: Drug Trafficking: Smuggling and Selling Illegal Drugs to Generate Income for the Regime

The Drug Trade in North Korea

The illicit drug trade is one of the many illegal businesses that support the communist dictatorship in North Korea. This subchapter aims to shed light on the extent and implications of drug trafficking in the country, providing valuable insights for diplomats and those interested in understanding North Korea's shadow economy.

Drug trafficking has become an increasingly lucrative enterprise for the regime, allowing them to generate substantial income while maintaining control over their population. The North Korean government has established a network of drug production and distribution channels, enabling them to smuggle and sell illegal drugs both domestically and internationally.

The regime's involvement in drug trafficking is primarily driven by its need for funds to sustain its oppressive rule. With limited access to legitimate sources of income, the communist dictatorship relies on illicit activities to finance its operations. The drug trade offers a reliable and profitable avenue for generating revenue, as the demand for narcotics continues to rise globally.

North Korea's geographical location and porous borders make it an ideal transit point for drug smuggling. The regime takes advantage of this by cultivating and processing drugs, such as methamphetamine, within its borders. These drugs are then smuggled into neighboring countries, including China and Japan, where they fetch high prices in the black market.

The consequences of the drug trade in North Korea extend beyond financial gains for the communist dictatorship. The proliferation of illicit drugs within the country has had devastating effects on its population, leading to addiction, health problems, and social decay. Moreover, the regime's involvement in drug trafficking undermines international efforts to combat the global drug trade, as it operates outside the reach of law enforcement agencies.

To address the issue of drug trafficking in North Korea, a coordinated international response is essential. Diplomats must work together to strengthen border controls, enhance intelligence sharing, and disrupt the financial networks that support the drug trade. Additionally, efforts should be made to provide support for addiction treatment and rehabilitation programs within the country, aiming to alleviate the suffering of the North Korean people.

In conclusion, the drug trade in North Korea plays a significant role in supporting the communist dictatorship. By engaging in drug trafficking, the regime not only generates substantial income but also perpetuates social harm and undermines global security. Diplomats must recognize the urgency of addressing this issue and work towards implementing comprehensive strategies to combat the drug trade and its implications for North Korea and the international community.

The Impact of Drug Trafficking on Society and the Regime

Drug trafficking has emerged as one of the most lucrative and consequential illegal businesses supporting the Communist dictatorship in North Korea. This subchapter aims to shed light on the far-reaching implications of this illicit trade, which extends beyond the boundaries of the authoritarian state. Addressed to diplomats and those interested in understanding the intricate workings of North Korea's shadow economy, this section explores the multifaceted impact of drug trafficking on both society and the regime itself.

First and foremost, drug trafficking poses a grave threat to the social fabric of North Korean society. As illicit drugs flood the markets, addiction rates surge, leading to a myriad of health and social issues. Families are torn apart, communities are destabilized, and individuals are trapped in a vicious cycle of substance abuse. This not only undermines the well-being and productivity of the population but also perpetuates a culture of dependency and despair.

Moreover, drug trafficking serves as a vital source of income for the Communist dictatorship. The revenue generated from the sale of illegal drugs is channeled to sustain the regime's oppressive apparatus. This financial lifeline enables the government to maintain its grip on power, fund its nuclear ambitions, and suppress dissent. The illicit drug trade, therefore, becomes an indispensable tool for the regime's survival and consolidation of power.

Furthermore, the international community must recognize the global implications of North Korea's involvement in drug trafficking. The influx of narcotics into neighboring countries not only fuels addiction and crime rates but also breeds instability and insecurity in the region. The profits derived from drug sales also facilitate the regime's engagement in other illicit activities, such as arms smuggling, counterfeit currency production, human trafficking, and cybercrime. These interconnected criminal enterprises heighten the risks faced by diplomats and threaten the stability of international relations.

To effectively combat the impact of drug trafficking, a comprehensive approach is crucial. Diplomats must collaborate with international organizations, law enforcement agencies, and regional partners to dismantle the networks that perpetuate this illicit trade. Addressing the root causes of drug addiction, investing in education and rehabilitation programs, and promoting alternative livelihoods are essential components of a long-term solution.

In conclusion, drug trafficking not only ravages the social fabric of North Korean society but also fuels the Communist dictatorship's grip on power. As diplomats and individuals concerned with the well-being of nations, it is imperative that we understand the profound consequences of this illicit trade. By relentlessly pursuing strategies to disrupt these criminal networks, we can mitigate the impact on society and work towards a more stable and prosperous future for North Korea and the international community at large.

Efforts to Combat Drug Trafficking in North Korea

Drug trafficking is one of the many illicit businesses that support the Communist dictatorship in North Korea. The regime relies on the smuggling and sale of illegal drugs to generate income and finance its oppressive rule. However, international efforts have been made to combat this nefarious activity and disrupt the flow of drugs within and beyond North Korea's borders.

Diplomats, concerned about the impact of drug trafficking on global security and the well-being of North Korean citizens, have been at the forefront of these efforts. Recognizing the grave consequences of drug trafficking, they have implemented various strategies to curb this illicit trade.

One of the primary approaches to combating drug trafficking in North Korea has been through international cooperation and intelligence sharing. Diplomats from different countries have joined forces to exchange information and coordinate their efforts. This collaboration has enabled the identification of drug trafficking routes, the apprehension of key players involved, and the interception of drug shipments.

Furthermore, diplomatic pressure has been exerted on North Korea to address the issue internally. Through diplomatic channels, countries have urged the North Korean regime to enforce stricter laws, enhance border control measures, and crack down on drug production and distribution networks. This pressure has resulted in some limited reforms and an increase in arrests and convictions related to drug trafficking.

Additionally, diplomatic initiatives have sought to raise awareness about the detrimental effects of drug trafficking on individuals and societies. By organizing educational programs and awareness campaigns, diplomats aim to discourage drug use within North Korea and reduce the demand for illicit drugs. They also collaborate with local communities and organizations to provide rehabilitation and support services for individuals affected by drug addiction.

Although these efforts have made some progress, drug trafficking remains a significant challenge in North Korea. The regime's involvement in this illicit trade, along with its repressive nature, makes it difficult to eradicate completely. However, diplomats continue to work tirelessly, employing various strategies and initiatives, to combat drug trafficking and dismantle the networks that support the Communist dictatorship.

By addressing drug trafficking, diplomats not only contribute to global security but also strive to alleviate the suffering of the North Korean people. Through international cooperation and persistent pressure, they aim to weaken the regime's grip on power and create a safer, drug-free North Korea.

Chapter 6: Human Trafficking: Illegal Trade of Humans for Forced Labor or Exploitation to Finance the Communist Dictatorship

The Dark Reality of Human Trafficking in North Korea

In the depths of North Korea's illicit businesses that support the communist dictatorship, a dark reality exists - the sinister web of human trafficking. This subchapter sheds light on this disturbing practice that plagues the nation, revealing the extent of its brutality and the dire consequences it has on innocent lives.

Human trafficking is the illegal trade of humans for forced labor or exploitation, serving as a lucrative means to finance the communist regime. The victims, often vulnerable individuals or families, are forcibly taken from their homes and subjected to a life of enslavement, abuse, and unimaginable suffering.

Countless men, women, and children fall victim to this heinous trade, with their hopes and dreams crushed under the weight of a merciless regime. They are forced into labor-intensive industries such as mining, construction, and agriculture, working under inhumane conditions for endless hours without any remuneration. Their lives are reduced to mere commodities, stripped of their freedom and dignity.

Women and young girls, in particular, face an even more harrowing fate. They are trafficked for sexual exploitation, becoming victims of a thriving underground market where their bodies are bought and sold like objects. These individuals are subjected to physical and psychological trauma, enduring a life of perpetual violence and degradation.

The North Korean government turns a blind eye to this illicit trade, allowing it to flourish under their watchful eye. The profits derived from human trafficking serve as a crucial source of income for the regime, further perpetuating their control over the country. The suffering of these victims is seen as collateral damage in their quest to maintain power.

As diplomats, it is our duty to confront this dark reality and work towards its eradication. By exposing the extent of human trafficking in North Korea, we can bring attention to the plight of these victims and rally international support for their rescue.

This subchapter serves as a call to action, urging diplomatic engagement and cooperation to dismantle the networks that facilitate this heinous trade. It is crucial to pressure the North Korean regime to address this issue and hold them accountable for their complicity in human rights abuses.

Only through a united front, with a relentless pursuit of justice, can we hope to bring an end to the dark reality of human trafficking in North Korea. Let us stand together, as diplomats, advocates for human rights, and champions of justice, to expose and dismantle the networks that perpetuate this abhorrent trade.

The Exploitation of North Korean Citizens

North Korea's illicit businesses play a crucial role in supporting the communist dictatorship, enabling it to maintain power and suppress its citizens. This subchapter sheds light on the extensive exploitation of North Korean citizens, revealing the dark underbelly of the regime's activities.

One of the communist regime's key sources of income is arms smuggling. The illegal trade of weapons not only sustains the regime but also poses a significant threat to regional stability. Diplomats need to be aware of this dangerous trade and take action to prevent the proliferation of weapons.

Counterfeit currency production is another insidious method employed by the regime to fund its activities. By printing fake money, the regime generates income while undermining the global financial system. Diplomats must be vigilant in detecting and combating this illicit practice.

Drug trafficking has become a lucrative business for the North Korean regime. Smuggling and selling illegal drugs not only generate income but also contribute to the social decay of societies worldwide. Diplomats should work together to disrupt the drug trade networks and protect vulnerable populations.

The communist dictatorship's involvement in human trafficking is deeply disturbing. Trafficking humans for forced labor or exploitation serves as a means to finance the regime's activities. Diplomats must prioritize combating this heinous crime and ensuring the protection of human rights.

Cybercrime has emerged as a significant tool for the regime to generate financial gain. By engaging in hacking, phishing, and other cyber activities, the regime poses a threat to global cybersecurity. Diplomats should collaborate to enhance cyber defenses and dismantle the regime's cyber networks.

The illegal sale of nuclear materials or technology by North Korea poses a grave threat to international security. Diplomats must actively counter nuclear proliferation and prevent the regime from profiting from these dangerous activities.

Wildlife smuggling, money laundering, illegal fishing, and illicit trade in natural resources all contribute to the regime's illicit economy. Diplomats must work together to combat these activities, which not only harm the environment but also perpetuate the suffering of North Korean citizens.

In conclusion, the exploitation of North Korean citizens is a crucial aspect of the communist regime's illicit businesses. Diplomats must be aware of these activities and take decisive action to dismantle the networks that sustain the regime's power. By addressing these issues, we can work towards a more just and prosperous future for the citizens of North Korea.

International Efforts to Combat Human Trafficking in North Korea

Human trafficking is one of the most egregious and inhumane crimes committed in North Korea, serving as a means to finance the communist dictatorship. The international community, including diplomats and concerned nations, has recognized the urgent need to combat this heinous practice and put an end to the suffering of countless individuals. Efforts to combat human trafficking in North Korea have been multifaceted, targeting both the supply and demand sides of this illegal trade.

On the supply side, various international organizations and governments have been actively involved in raising awareness, conducting investigations, and providing assistance to victims. Diplomats have been engaged in diplomatic dialogues and negotiations with the North Korean government to address this issue. They have consistently urged North Korea to take concrete steps to protect its citizens and bring the perpetrators to justice. Additionally, diplomatic efforts have focused on encouraging North Korea to cooperate with international organizations and share information on trafficking networks operating within its borders.

On the demand side, international efforts have aimed at increasing awareness and strengthening legislation against human trafficking.

Diplomats have played a crucial role in advocating for stricter laws and policies in their respective countries to discourage the demand for forced labor and exploitation. International cooperation in intelligence sharing and joint law enforcement operations has also been instrumental in disrupting the networks involved in trafficking individuals for financial gain.

Collaboration between governments, international organizations, and non-governmental organizations (NGOs) has been pivotal in providing support to victims of human trafficking in North Korea. These efforts include the provision of shelter, medical and psychological assistance, and vocational training to help survivors reintegrate into society. Diplomats have facilitated the coordination and funding of such initiatives, ensuring that resources are effectively allocated to maximize impact.

Despite the challenges posed by the secretive nature of North Korea's regime, concerted international efforts have yielded some progress in combating human trafficking. However, there is still much work to be done. Diplomats and the international community must continue to prioritize this issue, using their influence and diplomatic channels to pressure North Korea to take further action. Additionally, increased cooperation and information sharing among nations can help dismantle trafficking networks and disrupt the financing of the communist dictatorship.

In conclusion, the fight against human trafficking in North Korea requires a comprehensive and collaborative approach. Diplomats have a crucial role to play in advocating for stronger legislation, raising awareness, and coordinating international efforts. By addressing the root causes and dismantling the networks involved, the international community can work towards eradicating this horrific crime and ultimately contribute to building a more just and humane society in North Korea.

Chapter 7: Cybercrime: Involvement in Hacking, Phishing, and Other Cyber Activities for Financial Gain

The Growing Threat of Cybercrime in North Korea

In recent years, the world has witnessed a concerning rise in cybercrime activities, and North Korea has emerged as a prominent player in this nefarious realm. This subchapter aims to shed light on the growing threat of cybercrime originating from North Korea, which poses significant challenges to global security and stability.

North Korea's involvement in cybercrime can be traced back to its desperate need for funds to sustain its communist dictatorship. As economic sanctions have tightened around the country, the regime has turned to unconventional means to generate income, and cybercrime has become a lucrative avenue for them.

One of the primary cybercrime activities conducted by North Korea is hacking. The regime has developed sophisticated hacking units, such as the infamous Lazarus Group, which has been responsible for numerous high-profile cyberattacks targeting financial institutions, cryptocurrency exchanges, and government entities. These attacks not only result in financial gains for North Korea but also serve as a tool to destabilize other nations.

Phishing is another cybercrime method employed by North Korea. The regime utilizes deceptive emails and websites to trick unsuspecting individuals into revealing sensitive information or downloading malicious software, which enables them to gain unauthorized access to systems and networks. This tactic has been used to target diplomats and government officials, further highlighting the threat posed by North Korea's cyber activities.

Furthermore, North Korea's cybercriminals engage in cryptocurrency theft and extortion, exploiting the anonymity and decentralized nature of digital currencies. They have been involved in various ransomware attacks, holding organizations hostage until a ransom is paid in cryptocurrencies, thereby enabling the regime to accumulate funds covertly.

The international community, particularly diplomats, must recognize the severity of the threat posed by North Korea's cybercriminal activities. It is imperative to develop robust cybersecurity measures, enhance information sharing, and establish international cooperation to effectively combat this growing menace.

Diplomatic efforts should also focus on pressuring North Korea to cease its cybercrime activities through economic sanctions and diplomatic channels. Additionally, engaging with other countries affected by North Korea's cyber operations can foster collaborative strategies to counter this threat effectively.

In conclusion, North Korea's involvement in cybercrime represents a significant and evolving threat to global security. Diplomats must prioritize addressing this issue, recognizing the interconnected nature of cyber threats and the potential implications they have on not only financial systems but also international relations. By tackling cybercrime head-on, the international community can curtail North Korea's illicit activities and safeguard the integrity of the digital realm.

The Role of Cyber Activities in Financing the Regime

In the modern era, cyber activities have become an increasingly popular method for illicit businesses to finance their operations. This subchapter will shed light on the significant role of cyber activities in supporting the Communist dictatorship in North Korea. Addressed to diplomats and those interested in North Korea's illegal businesses, this section aims to provide a comprehensive understanding of the various cyber activities employed by the regime.

Cybercrime has emerged as a lucrative venture for the North Korean regime, enabling them to generate substantial funds while maintaining anonymity. Hacking, phishing, and other cyber activities have become their weapon of choice in acquiring financial gain. By targeting financial institutions, corporations, and even individuals, North Korea's cyber operatives have successfully obtained vast amounts of money through fraudulent means.

The regime's involvement in counterfeit currency production is another alarming aspect of their illicit businesses. By printing fake money, they can inject it into legitimate economies, further destabilizing financial systems. These counterfeit notes are often of such high quality that they can easily pass undetected, enabling the regime to fund its activities while evading detection.

Drug trafficking has long been associated with organized crime, and the North Korean regime has not shied away from engaging in this illicit trade. Smuggling and selling illegal drugs provide a substantial source of income for the regime, which they exploit to further their communist dictatorship. The sale of drugs not only generates revenue but also serves as a means of exerting control over vulnerable populations.

Human trafficking is another abhorrent practice employed by the regime to finance their activities. The illegal trade of humans for forced labor or exploitation not only generates income but also instills fear and control over the population. This heinous trade ensures a constant flow of funds, allowing the regime to maintain its grip on power.

Nuclear proliferation, wildlife smuggling, money laundering, illegal fishing, and illicit trade in natural resources are additional avenues through which the North Korean regime finances its communist dictatorship. These activities exploit global vulnerabilities, taking advantage of weak regulations and corrupt networks to generate substantial profits.

In conclusion, cyber activities play a pivotal role in financing the Communist dictatorship in North Korea. The regime's involvement in hacking, counterfeit currency production, drug trafficking, human trafficking, and other illicit activities provides a constant stream of funds to further their oppressive regime. It is imperative for diplomats and those concerned with North Korea's illegal businesses to understand and combat these cyber activities to dismantle the financial support system that sustains the communist dictatorship.

Strategies to Combat North Korean Cybercrime

In recent years, North Korean cybercrime has emerged as a significant threat to global security and stability. The regime's involvement in hacking, phishing, and other cyber activities for financial gain has become a primary means for the communist dictatorship to generate income and fund its illicit businesses. As diplomats, it is vital for us to understand and address this issue in order to protect our nations and uphold international law.

One of the most effective strategies to combat North Korean cybercrime is through international cooperation. Diplomatic efforts should focus on fostering collaboration between countries to share intelligence, coordinate investigations, and develop joint strategies to disrupt and dismantle cybercriminal networks. By working together, we can enhance our collective ability to detect and respond to North Korean cyber threats.

Another key approach is to strengthen our cybersecurity defenses. Diplomats should advocate for the implementation of robust cybersecurity measures in their respective countries, including regular updates of software and operating systems, strong password policies, and employee training on recognizing and responding to phishing attempts. By fortifying our defenses, we can mitigate the likelihood of successful cyber attacks.

Furthermore, engaging with the private sector is crucial in combating North Korean cybercrime. Diplomats should encourage partnerships between governments and technology companies, financial institutions, and cybersecurity firms to share information, develop innovative solutions, and enhance the resilience of critical infrastructure. Collaborative initiatives can help identify and neutralize cyber threats more effectively.

In addition to these measures, diplomatic efforts should focus on imposing stricter sanctions on North Korea. By targeting the regime's financial networks and restricting its access to international banking systems, we can disrupt the flow of funds that sustain their cybercriminal activities. Diplomats should also engage with countries that host North Korean cyber actors and advocate for their cooperation in apprehending and prosecuting those involved in cybercrime.

Lastly, increasing public awareness and education on North Korean cyber threats is crucial. Diplomats should work with their governments and international organizations to develop campaigns that educate individuals and businesses about the risks of cybercrime and provide guidance on how to protect themselves. By fostering a culture of cyber resilience, we can empower individuals and organizations to become active participants in combating North Korean cyber threats.

In conclusion, addressing North Korean cybercrime requires a multi-faceted approach that involves international cooperation, strengthening cybersecurity defenses, engaging the private sector, imposing stricter sanctions, and increasing public awareness. As diplomats, it is our responsibility to champion these strategies and work collectively to combat the illicit businesses supporting the communist dictatorship in North Korea.

Chapter 8: Nuclear Proliferation: Illegal Sale of Nuclear Materials or Technology to Support North Korea's Nuclear Program

The Nuclear Program in North Korea

North Korea's nuclear program remains one of the most pressing concerns for the international community. This subchapter delves into the illicit activities associated with the program, shedding light on the shadowy economy that sustains the communist dictatorship. Diplomats and those interested in understanding the intricate web of North Korea's illegal businesses will find this section particularly insightful.

The regime's pursuit of nuclear weapons has been a source of tension and instability in the region for decades. This chapter explores the various aspects of North Korea's nuclear program, including the illicit sale of nuclear materials and technology. The regime, driven by the desire for power and influence, has engaged in clandestine transactions to acquire the necessary resources to advance its nuclear ambitions.

The subchapter also uncovers the link between the nuclear program and the broader illicit activities that support the communist dictatorship. Arms smuggling, for instance, plays a pivotal role in financing the regime's nuclear agenda. The illegal trade of weapons not only provides revenue but also strengthens North Korea's military capabilities, enabling it to further its nuclear ambitions.

Another illicit business explored in this section is counterfeit currency production. The regime has resorted to printing fake money as a means to fund its nuclear program. This nefarious activity not only destabilizes global financial systems but also reveals the extent to which the communist dictatorship will go to secure funds for its nuclear endeavors.

Drug trafficking is another avenue through which the regime generates income for its nuclear program. Involvement in the smuggling and sale of illegal drugs not only poses a threat to public health but also highlights the regime's willingness to exploit vulnerable populations to finance its nuclear pursuits.

The subchapter also delves into other illicit activities, such as human trafficking, cybercrime, wildlife smuggling, money laundering, illegal fishing, and illicit trade in natural resources. Each of these activities plays a significant role in propping up the North Korean regime and supporting its nuclear program.

In conclusion, this subchapter provides a comprehensive overview of the nuclear program in North Korea and its connection to the shadow economy that sustains the communist dictatorship. Diplomats and those interested in understanding the inner workings of North Korea's illicit businesses will find this section invaluable in unraveling the complex web of activities that support the regime's nuclear ambitions. By shedding light on these illicit activities, we hope to foster a greater understanding of the challenges posed by North Korea's nuclear program and the need for international cooperation to address this pressing issue.

The Illicit Trade in Nuclear Materials and Technology

"The Illicit Trade in Nuclear Materials and Technology"

Introduction:

In the global landscape of clandestine activities, few threats loom as large as the illicit trade in nuclear materials and technology. This subchapter sheds light on this grave concern, specifically within the context of North Korea's illicit businesses supporting the communist dictatorship.

Addressing a distinguished audience of diplomats, we delve into the intricate web of dark operations that perpetuate the North Korean regime's nuclear ambitions.

North Korea's Nuclear Program:

North Korea's relentless pursuit of nuclear weapons has posed a grave challenge to regional stability and international security. This subchapter aims to provide insight into the illicit trade networks that enable the regime's nuclear proliferation activities. By understanding the mechanisms, motivations, and consequences of this trade, diplomats can better formulate strategies to curb its growth and protect global peace.

The Nexus of Nuclear Proliferation and Illicit Trade:

The illegal sale of nuclear materials and technology is undeniably intertwined with North Korea's nuclear program. Through covert channels, the regime procures and distributes these components to advance its capabilities. Diplomats must grasp the gravity of this trade, as it represents a direct threat to global non-proliferation efforts and the stability of the Korean Peninsula.

The Dangers and Consequences:

The illicit trade in nuclear materials and technology poses substantial risks on multiple fronts. Not only does it bolster North Korea's nuclear program, but it also increases the likelihood of these materials falling into the wrong hands, potentially enabling rogue states or non-state actors to develop their own nuclear capabilities. Diplomats must recognize the urgency to dismantle these networks to safeguard global security.

Countering the Illicit Trade:

Addressing this grave challenge requires a multi-faceted approach. Diplomats must collaborate closely to enhance intelligence sharing, strengthen export controls, and promote international cooperation. By disrupting the illicit trade networks, the global community can effectively impede the growth of North Korea's nuclear program and protect against the proliferation of these dangerous materials.

Conclusion:

The illicit trade in nuclear materials and technology is a pressing concern, particularly within the context of North Korea's illicit businesses supporting the communist dictatorship. Diplomats must recognize the gravity of this threat and actively work towards dismantling the networks that enable it. By doing so, they can lay the groundwork for a more secure and stable world, free from the specter of nuclear proliferation.

The Global Response to North Korea's Nuclear Proliferation

In recent years, the international community has been grappling with the complex issue of North Korea's nuclear proliferation. This subchapter explores the global response to this alarming threat and sheds light on the various measures taken to address the issue.

Diplomats, who are at the forefront of international relations, play a crucial role in formulating and implementing strategies to curb North Korea's illicit activities. They are not only responsible for maintaining diplomatic relations but also for safeguarding global security and stability. Understanding the intricacies of North Korea's illegal businesses supporting the communist dictatorship is essential for them to effectively combat these activities.

One of the most pressing concerns is the illicit trade in nuclear materials and technology. North Korea's nuclear program poses a significant threat to regional and global security. Diplomats have been engaged in extensive negotiations and dialogues to persuade North Korea to abandon its nuclear ambitions. The imposition of economic sanctions by the United Nations Security Council has been a key tool used to pressure the regime into compliance. Efforts to enforce these sanctions and prevent the proliferation of nuclear materials continue to be a priority for diplomats worldwide.

Arms smuggling is another illegal trade that supports the North Korean regime. Diplomats have been working tirelessly to strengthen international arms control mechanisms and increase cooperation between countries to prevent the illicit trade of weapons. Sharing intelligence, conducting joint operations, and implementing stricter export controls have been some of the measures taken to counter this threat.

The production of counterfeit currency is yet another illicit business that funds the communist dictatorship. Diplomats have been collaborating with international law enforcement agencies to dismantle counterfeit currency networks and disrupt their operations. Enhancing cooperation and intelligence sharing between countries has proved instrumental in identifying and apprehending individuals involved in this criminal activity.

The global response to North Korea's nuclear proliferation also encompasses efforts to combat drug trafficking, human trafficking, cybercrime, wildlife smuggling, money laundering, illegal fishing, and illicit trade in natural resources. Diplomats have been actively involved in initiatives aimed at raising awareness, strengthening legislation, and facilitating international cooperation to tackle these issues.

In conclusion, the global response to North Korea's nuclear proliferation and its illicit businesses supporting the communist dictatorship requires a multifaceted approach. Diplomats play a vital role in formulating and implementing strategies to counter these threats. By fostering international cooperation, sharing intelligence, and implementing stricter regulations, diplomats are working towards dismantling the shadow economy that sustains the North Korean regime. It is through their relentless efforts that the international community aims to achieve lasting peace and security in the region.

Chapter 9: Wildlife Smuggling: Illegal Trade of Endangered Species and Animal Products for Profit

The Exploitation of North Korea's Wildlife

North Korea's illicit businesses to support the communist dictatorship are not limited to arms smuggling, counterfeit currency production, drug trafficking, human trafficking, cybercrime, nuclear proliferation, money laundering, illegal fishing, and illicit trade in natural resources. They also extend to the illegal trade of wildlife, which has become a lucrative endeavor for the regime.

Wildlife smuggling, driven by greed and the insatiable demand for exotic animals and their products, has reached alarming levels in North Korea. The communist dictatorship has turned a blind eye to this illicit trade, allowing criminal networks to flourish and profit at the expense of the country's unique biodiversity.

Endangered species, including tigers, rhinos, pangolins, and elephants, are among the victims of this illicit trade. Their body parts, such as skin, bones, and horns, are highly sought after in black markets across Asia and beyond. North Korea's wildlife smuggling operations have established networks that span borders, making it difficult for law enforcement agencies to tackle this issue effectively.

The exploitation of North Korea's wildlife is not only an ecological disaster but also a moral outrage. It highlights the regime's callous disregard for the environment and its willingness to profit from the suffering and extinction of endangered species. Diplomats and concerned citizens must unite to address this issue and put pressure on the North Korean regime to take immediate action.

Efforts to combat wildlife smuggling should include strengthening international cooperation, implementing stricter regulations, and providing resources for law enforcement agencies to disrupt these criminal networks. Diplomatic pressure can play a crucial role in urging North Korea to strengthen its own laws and enforcement mechanisms to combat this illicit trade.

Moreover, raising public awareness about the consequences of wildlife smuggling is paramount. By educating consumers about the impact of their choices, we can reduce the demand for illegal wildlife products and undermine the profitability of this illicit trade.

In conclusion, the exploitation of North Korea's wildlife is a grave concern that must be addressed by the international community. Diplomats have a crucial role to play in advocating for stronger regulations, international cooperation, and public awareness campaigns to combat wildlife smuggling. By standing united against this illicit trade, we can protect precious species, preserve biodiversity, and send a strong message to the North Korean regime that their actions will not go unnoticed or unpunished.

The Connection Between Wildlife Smuggling and the Regime

Wildlife smuggling, also known as the illegal trade of endangered species and animal products, has emerged as a significant illicit business supporting the communist dictatorship in North Korea. This subchapter aims to shed light on the intricate connection between wildlife smuggling and the regime's illicit activities, providing valuable insights for diplomats and individuals interested in understanding the shadow economy of North Korea.

The communist dictatorship in North Korea has long been involved in various illegal businesses to finance its oppressive regime. From arms smuggling to counterfeit currency production, drug trafficking to human trafficking, the regime has shown its willingness to engage in any illicit activity that generates income. However, wildlife smuggling has recently gained momentum and has become an integral part of the regime's illicit businesses.

The exploitation of wildlife resources for financial gain has become increasingly attractive for the regime due to the high demand for exotic animals and animal products in international markets. North Korea's geographical location and porous borders have made it an ideal transit point for smuggling wildlife across Asia, with destinations ranging from China to Southeast Asian countries.

The regime's involvement in wildlife smuggling can be attributed to various factors. Firstly, the profitability of this illicit trade cannot be underestimated. The demand for rare animals, such as tigers, rhinos, and pangolins, coupled with the scarcity of these species, drives up their prices significantly. The regime has realized the potential financial windfall that can be obtained from exploiting these resources.

Secondly, wildlife smuggling offers a low-risk opportunity for the regime to generate income. Compared to other illicit activities, such as drug trafficking or arms smuggling, wildlife smuggling often attracts less attention from law enforcement agencies. The regime can capitalize on this by channeling its resources towards this relatively safer endeavor.

Lastly, the connection between wildlife smuggling and the regime's larger agenda cannot be ignored. North Korea's nuclear program and its quest for international recognition have come at a high cost. Engaging in illegal wildlife trade provides an additional source of funding to support these endeavors, allowing the regime to maintain its grip on power and pursue its objectives.

In conclusion, wildlife smuggling has become an integral part of North Korea's shadow economy, supporting the communist dictatorship in various ways. Its profitability, low-risk nature, and alignment with the regime's larger agenda make it an attractive illicit business. Diplomats, as well as those interested in understanding North Korea's illegal activities, must recognize the connection between wildlife smuggling and the regime, as it sheds light on the complex and multifaceted nature of the shadow economy that sustains the communist dictatorship.

International Initiatives to Combat Wildlife Smuggling in North Korea

Introduction:

North Korea's illicit businesses play a significant role in supporting the communist dictatorship, with various activities such as arms smuggling, counterfeit currency production, drug trafficking, human trafficking, cybercrime, nuclear proliferation, money laundering, illegal fishing, and illicit trade in natural resources. Among these illegal practices, wildlife smuggling has gained attention due to its detrimental impact on biodiversity and the global fight against illegal wildlife trade. This subchapter explores international initiatives aimed at combating wildlife smuggling in North Korea, highlighting the efforts made by the global community to address this pressing issue.

Partnerships and Collaborations:

Diplomatic efforts have been crucial in establishing partnerships and collaborations to combat wildlife smuggling in North Korea. Governments, international organizations, and non-governmental organizations (NGOs) have joined forces to tackle this issue. The United Nations Office on Drugs and Crime (UNODC) has been instrumental in coordinating efforts and providing technical assistance to member states. Collaborative efforts with INTERPOL, the World Customs Organization, and the International Consortium on Combating Wildlife Crime (ICCWC) have also strengthened the fight against wildlife smuggling.

Capacity Building and Training:

To combat wildlife smuggling effectively, capacity building and training programs have been introduced. These initiatives aim to enhance the skills and knowledge of law enforcement officials in identifying and combating wildlife smuggling networks. Training workshops and seminars provide practical tools, including techniques for detecting and investigating wildlife smuggling cases, sharing intelligence, and coordinating efforts across borders.

Intelligence Sharing and Cooperation:

International intelligence sharing and cooperation have proven vital in combating wildlife smuggling in North Korea. Intelligence agencies and law enforcement bodies exchange information and collaborate on investigations to dismantle smuggling networks. The sharing of best practices, information on known criminals, and intelligence on smuggling routes and techniques enables a more coordinated and effective response.

Awareness and Public Outreach:

Raising awareness among the general public is crucial to combat wildlife smuggling. Diplomats have a pivotal role in advocating for the protection of endangered species and promoting responsible consumer behavior. By engaging with local communities, organizing educational campaigns, and leveraging social media, diplomats can encourage public support and denounce the illegal trade in wildlife products.

Conclusion:

International initiatives to combat wildlife smuggling in North Korea have made significant strides in addressing this illegal trade. Through partnerships, capacity building, intelligence sharing, and public outreach, the global community is working towards dismantling smuggling networks and protecting endangered species. Diplomats play a critical role in advocating for stronger enforcement measures, fostering international cooperation, and raising awareness among the public. By continuing these efforts, we can contribute to the preservation of biodiversity and undermine the financial resources that support the communist dictatorship in North Korea.

Chapter 10: Money Laundering: Using Illegal Means to Make Illicit Funds Appear Legitimate

Money Laundering Networks in North Korea

North Korea's illicit businesses have long been a source of concern for the international community, and money laundering plays a crucial role in sustaining the Communist dictatorship. This subchapter will delve into the intricate networks involved in money laundering within North Korea, shedding light on the methods employed and the impact they have on the country's economy and political stability.

Money laundering is the process of disguising the origins of illegally obtained funds, making them appear legitimate. In North Korea, this practice is not only widespread but also intricately woven into the fabric of the regime's illicit activities. By laundering money, the Communist dictatorship is able to sustain its operations, evade international sanctions, and further its nuclear ambitions.

One of the key aspects of North Korea's money laundering networks is their global reach. These networks span across various countries, utilizing offshore accounts, shell companies, and complex financial transactions to obscure the true source of funds. Diplomats need to be aware of the intricacies of these networks, as they have the potential to undermine global financial systems and contribute to the regime's illegal activities.

Furthermore, these networks are often interconnected with other illicit businesses that support the Communist dictatorship. Arms smuggling, counterfeit currency production, drug trafficking, human trafficking, cybercrime, and illicit trade in natural resources all contribute to the money laundering networks. By understanding the interplay between these different illegal activities, diplomats can develop comprehensive strategies to combat them effectively.

The consequences of money laundering in North Korea are far-reaching. It not only perpetuates the regime's oppressive rule but also poses significant risks to global security and stability. The funds generated through money laundering enable the regime to finance its nuclear program, proliferate weapons, and engage in other illicit activities that threaten regional and international peace.

To counter these money laundering networks, a coordinated international effort is crucial. Diplomats must collaborate with law enforcement agencies, financial institutions, and other relevant stakeholders to disrupt the flow of illicit funds and hold those involved accountable. Additionally, targeted sanctions and enhanced regulatory measures can help restrict the regime's access to the global financial system.

In conclusion, money laundering networks in North Korea play a pivotal role in sustaining the Communist dictatorship and enabling its illicit activities. Diplomats must be well-informed about these networks and their interconnectedness with other illegal businesses. By addressing the issue of money laundering, the international community can undermine the regime's financial capabilities and work towards a more stable and secure future for North Korea and the world at large.

Techniques and Methods Used in Money Laundering

Money laundering is a crucial aspect of North Korea's illicit businesses, enabling the communist dictatorship to disguise the origins of their illicit funds and integrate them into the legitimate economy. This subchapter will delve into the various techniques and methods employed by the regime to launder money, providing insights into their sophisticated operations.

One prevalent method employed by North Korea is the use of shell companies and front businesses. These entities serve as a facade, allowing the regime to obscure the true ownership and control of their illicit funds. These shell companies engage in legitimate transactions, creating a veneer of legality and making it difficult for authorities to trace the money back to its criminal origins.

Another technique utilized by the regime is trade-based money laundering. North Korea leverages its extensive network of legal and illegal trade routes to artificially inflate the value of goods, facilitating the movement of illicit funds across borders. By manipulating invoices, misrepresenting the value of goods, and engaging in over and under-invoicing, the regime can legitimize their illegal proceeds.

The use of offshore accounts and complex financial structures is also prevalent in North Korea's money laundering operations. By establishing accounts in jurisdictions with lax regulations and banking secrecy, such as offshore tax havens, the regime can further obscure their financial activities. They often employ layering techniques, involving multiple transactions and intermediaries, to make it increasingly difficult for authorities to follow the money trail.

Furthermore, North Korea actively exploits the cryptocurrency market for money laundering purposes. The anonymous nature of cryptocurrencies provides an ideal platform for the regime to move illicit funds across borders without detection. They engage in mixing services, tumblers, and other techniques to obfuscate the origin and destination of the funds, effectively laundering their money in the digital realm.

It is crucial for diplomats and those interested in North Korea's illegal businesses to understand these techniques and methods used in money laundering. By comprehending these strategies, authorities can develop effective countermeasures to disrupt the regime's illicit financial networks. This knowledge can assist in building international collaborations and implementing robust regulatory frameworks to combat money laundering and ultimately undermine the support for the communist dictatorship.

Efforts to Combat Money Laundering in North Korea

Money laundering is a critical issue that supports the illicit businesses of North Korea and enables the communist dictatorship to continue its oppressive regime. Diplomats play a crucial role in understanding and addressing this problem, as they hold the power to implement policies and engage in international cooperation to combat money laundering effectively.

North Korea's illicit businesses are diverse and extensive, ranging from arms smuggling and counterfeit currency production to drug trafficking and human trafficking. The communist regime also engages in cybercrime, nuclear proliferation, wildlife smuggling, illegal fishing, and illicit trade in natural resources. These illegal activities generate significant profits, which are then funneled through complex money laundering networks to make them appear legitimate.

To counter this challenge, diplomats must collaborate with international organizations, financial institutions, and law enforcement agencies to strengthen anti-money laundering measures. This would involve implementing stricter regulations, improving information sharing mechanisms, and enhancing the capacity of financial institutions to detect suspicious transactions.

One effective approach is to focus on disrupting the financial networks that facilitate money laundering in North Korea. This could be achieved by imposing targeted sanctions on individuals, entities, and financial institutions involved in these illicit activities. It is essential to identify and freeze assets linked to money laundering and ensure that these funds are repurposed to support humanitarian efforts within North Korea.

Furthermore, raising awareness among the international community is crucial in combating money laundering in North Korea. Diplomats can play a pivotal role in educating governments, businesses, and individuals about the risks associated with engaging in financial transactions that may indirectly support the communist regime. By highlighting the severe consequences of money laundering, such as the perpetuation of human rights abuses and the threat to regional security, diplomats can encourage greater vigilance and adherence to anti-money laundering measures.

In conclusion, combating money laundering in North Korea requires a comprehensive and collaborative effort from diplomats, international organizations, and financial institutions. By strengthening regulations, disrupting financial networks, and raising awareness, significant progress can be made in dismantling the illicit businesses that sustain the communist dictatorship. This, in turn, will contribute to fostering a more just and prosperous North Korea, free from the shackles of illicit activities.

Chapter 11: Illegal Fishing: Engaging in Unregulated and Illegal Fishing Activities to Generate Income

The Illegal Fishing Industry in North Korea

In the dark underbelly of North Korea's illicit businesses, the illegal fishing industry stands out as a major contributor to the communist dictatorship's coffers. This subchapter sheds light on the clandestine operations of this industry and its detrimental impact on the global marine ecosystem.

North Korea's geographical location, with its extensive coastline along the Yellow Sea and the Sea of Japan, provides ample opportunities for fishing. However, the regime's desperate need for foreign currency has pushed them to exploit this resource ruthlessly and without regard for international laws and regulations.

Illegal fishing vessels, often operating under the guise of legal fishing operations, are equipped with advanced technology and weaponry to evade detection and capture. These vessels venture into foreign waters, targeting valuable species such as squid, crab, and tuna, depleting their populations and disrupting the delicate balance of marine ecosystems.

The diplomatic community must be aware of the link between the illegal fishing industry and North Korea's support for the communist dictatorship. Proceeds from these activities directly fund the regime's oppressive machinery, enabling it to maintain control over its people and pursue its dangerous nuclear ambitions.

Moreover, the illegal fishing industry is intertwined with other illicit businesses, such as arms smuggling, counterfeit currency production, and drug trafficking. Diplomats must understand the interconnectedness of these activities, as they collectively enable the regime to sustain its autocratic rule.

The international community must take a united stand against the illegal fishing industry in North Korea. Strengthening maritime security and surveillance measures, imposing stricter sanctions, and collaborating with neighboring countries to combat this illegal trade are essential steps in curbing the regime's illicit activities.

Additionally, diplomats should support initiatives aimed at raising awareness about the environmental consequences of illegal fishing. By highlighting the devastating impact on marine ecosystems and endangered species, we can foster a sense of responsibility among nations to protect our shared natural resources.

In conclusion, illegal fishing in North Korea serves as a critical revenue stream for the communist dictatorship, perpetuating its oppressive regime and jeopardizing marine ecosystems. Diplomats play a crucial role in addressing this issue, as they possess the power to shape international policies and foster cooperation among nations. By taking a firm stance against the illegal fishing industry, we can contribute to dismantling the shadow economy that supports the North Korean regime and safeguarding the future of our oceans.

The Environmental and Economic Consequences of Illegal Fishing

Illegal fishing has emerged as one of the most pressing concerns in today's global economy, with far-reaching consequences for both the environment and the economy. This subchapter focuses on the environmental and economic ramifications of illegal fishing, particularly in the context of North Korea's illicit businesses supporting the communist dictatorship.

Illegal fishing not only depletes fish stocks but also disrupts delicate marine ecosystems. As North Korea engages in unregulated and illegal fishing activities, it puts immense pressure on already vulnerable fish populations, leading to their rapid decline. This depletion disrupts the delicate balance of marine ecosystems, impacting the entire food chain and threatening the survival of numerous marine species.

Furthermore, illegal fishing has severe economic consequences. By engaging in unregulated fishing practices, North Korea's illegal fishing industry undermines the livelihoods of legitimate fishermen and fishing communities around the world. The overfishing and depletion of fish stocks caused by illegal fishing ultimately leads to decreased catches and reduced incomes for law-abiding fishermen, exacerbating poverty and food insecurity in many coastal communities.

Moreover, the economic repercussions of illegal fishing extend beyond the fishing industry itself. As illegal fishers continue to exploit marine resources, they also disrupt the tourism industry, which heavily relies on the preservation of marine ecosystems. The degradation of coral reefs, depletion of fish stocks, and destruction of marine habitats caused by illegal fishing deter tourists, resulting in significant economic losses for coastal regions dependent on tourism revenue.

Addressing the environmental and economic consequences of illegal fishing requires concerted international efforts. Diplomats and stakeholders must collaborate to strengthen enforcement mechanisms, enhance regional cooperation, and promote sustainable fishing practices. By implementing stricter regulations, increasing surveillance and monitoring capabilities, and imposing severe penalties for illegal fishing activities, the international community can deter illegal fishers and protect marine ecosystems.

Moreover, sustainable fishing initiatives, such as promoting responsible fishing practices, supporting small-scale fishermen, and fostering community-based management systems, can help restore fish stocks and revitalize fishing communities. By investing in these initiatives, diplomats can contribute to the sustainable development of coastal regions, ensuring the long-term prosperity of both the environment and the economy.

In conclusion, the environmental and economic consequences of illegal fishing are significant and far-reaching. As North Korea's illicit businesses support the communist dictatorship, it is crucial for diplomats and stakeholders to address this issue effectively. By combating illegal fishing, we can protect marine ecosystems, preserve fish stocks, and promote sustainable economic development in coastal communities worldwide.

International Efforts to Combat Illegal Fishing in North Korea

Illegal fishing has become a significant issue in North Korea, with the communist dictatorship engaging in unregulated and illegal fishing activities to generate income. This subchapter aims to shed light on the international efforts being made to combat this illicit business and its impact on North Korea's economy and the global fishing industry.

Illegal fishing in North Korea poses a serious threat to the sustainability of marine resources and undermines the livelihoods of legitimate fishermen in neighboring countries. Diplomats and stakeholders concerned with North Korea's illegal businesses supporting the communist dictatorship must recognize the importance of addressing this issue to promote regional stability and environmental sustainability.

Several international initiatives have been established to combat illegal fishing in North Korea. The United Nations has played a crucial role in coordinating efforts through its agencies like the Food and Agriculture Organization (FAO) and the United Nations Office on Drugs and Crime (UNODC). These organizations work closely with member states to strengthen legal frameworks and enhance enforcement capacities to tackle illegal fishing.

Regional collaborations have also been instrumental in combating illegal fishing in North Korea. The Association of Southeast Asian Nations (ASEAN) and the North Pacific Fisheries Commission (NPFC) have implemented measures to promote sustainable fishing practices and enhance surveillance and enforcement capabilities. These initiatives aim to curb illegal fishing activities in North Korean waters and prevent the smuggling of illegally caught fish into international markets.

Furthermore, international NGOs and non-profit organizations are actively involved in raising awareness about the consequences of illegal fishing in North Korea. They provide technical assistance, training, and capacity-building programs to support the development of sustainable fishing practices. These efforts contribute to empowering local communities and promoting alternative livelihoods, which ultimately reduce the reliance on illegal fishing.

While progress has been made, combating illegal fishing in North Korea remains a complex challenge. The clandestine nature of these activities and North Korea's limited transparency pose significant obstacles. Therefore, a comprehensive approach that combines law enforcement, intelligence sharing, and engagement with North Korean authorities is essential to effectively address this issue.

In conclusion, international efforts to combat illegal fishing in North Korea are vital to protect marine resources, promote regional stability, and address the illicit businesses supporting the communist dictatorship. Diplomats and stakeholders must continue to collaborate, share information, and support initiatives that enhance surveillance, enforcement, and sustainable fishing practices. By doing so, we can work towards a future where the fishing industry in North Korea operates within legal and sustainable frameworks, benefiting both the local communities and the global fishing industry.

Chapter 12: Illicit Trade in Natural Resources: Smuggling of Minerals, Timber, or Other Natural Resources to Support the Communist Dictatorship

The Exploitation of North Korea's Natural Resources

North Korea's illicit businesses play a crucial role in supporting the communist dictatorship, enabling it to maintain its oppressive regime. Among these illegal activities, the exploitation of the country's natural resources stands out as a major source of income. This subchapter delves into the shadowy world of North Korea's illicit trade in minerals, timber, and other natural resources, shedding light on the dark practices that sustain the regime.

The communist dictatorship, facing international sanctions and isolated from the global economy, has turned to illegal means to generate revenue. Exploiting the abundance of natural resources within its borders has become a lucrative avenue. North Korea's mountains are rich in minerals, including coal, iron ore, gold, and rare earth elements. The regime has capitalized on these resources, illicitly extracting and smuggling them to foreign markets.

Mineral smuggling not only provides the regime with much-needed funds but also serves as a way to circumvent international sanctions. By clandestinely exporting minerals, North Korea evades the watchful eye of the international community, ensuring a steady flow of income to sustain its oppressive rule. Timber, too, has become a valuable resource for the regime, with illegal logging rampant across the country. The illicit trade in timber further bolsters the regime's financial resources.

This subchapter also explores the environmental impact of North Korea's illicit trade in natural resources. The communist dictatorship's disregard for sustainable practices and lack of regulations has led to severe deforestation, soil erosion, and water pollution. The exploitation of natural resources has not only contributed to the regime's financial survival but has also come at a significant cost to the environment and the well-being of the North Korean people.

Diplomats reading this book will gain a comprehensive understanding of the extent to which the communist dictatorship exploits its natural resources to maintain its grip on power. They will also recognize the environmental implications and the urgent need for international cooperation to curb these illicit activities. By shedding light on this aspect of North Korea's shadow economy, diplomats can better comprehend the interconnectedness of various illicit businesses that support the regime, such as arms smuggling, counterfeit currency production, drug trafficking, and human trafficking.

It is imperative that the international community continues to exert pressure on North Korea to halt the exploitation of natural resources and other illicit activities. By doing so, diplomats and concerned global citizens can contribute to the ultimate goal of dismantling the communist dictatorship and bringing about a brighter future for the oppressed people of North Korea.

The Role of Illicit Trade in Financing the Regime

Introduction:

In the secretive and isolated nation of North Korea, the communist dictatorship relies heavily on illicit trade to sustain its regime. This subchapter aims to shed light on the various illegal businesses that support the North Korean government and the detrimental consequences they have on both the country and the international community. Addressed to diplomats, this chapter will explore the different facets of illicit trade, highlighting the ways in which it funds the oppressive regime.

Arms smuggling:

One of the primary sources of income for the North Korean regime is arms smuggling. By engaging in the illegal trade of weapons, the communist government can acquire the funds necessary to sustain its military apparatus and nuclear program. The proliferation of weapons poses a significant threat not only to regional stability but also to the global community.

Counterfeit currency production:

Another illicit business conducted by North Korea is the production of counterfeit currency. By printing fake money, the regime generates substantial profits while also destabilizing global economies. Counterfeit currency not only undermines the integrity of financial systems but also facilitates illicit activities such as drug trafficking and money laundering.

Drug trafficking:

North Korea is notorious for its involvement in drug trafficking, smuggling and selling illegal drugs to generate income for the regime. The production and distribution of drugs, such as methamphetamines, not only provide significant financial resources to the regime but also contribute to the drug epidemic faced by neighboring countries. The consequences of drug trafficking on public health and security cannot be underestimated.

Human trafficking:

The regime's involvement in human trafficking is a grave violation of human rights. By engaging in the illegal trade of humans for forced labor or exploitation, North Korea finances its communist dictatorship. This abhorrent practice not only enslaves innocent individuals but also perpetuates the cycle of oppression and misery experienced by the North Korean people.

Cybercrime:

North Korea's involvement in cybercrime, including hacking, phishing, and other cyber activities, serves as an additional revenue stream for the regime. By targeting financial institutions, corporations, and governments, the regime gains access to significant funds, further bolstering its oppressive rule. The international community must remain vigilant against these cyber threats.

Conclusion:

The role of illicit trade in financing the North Korean regime cannot be understated. From arms smuggling to drug trafficking, human trafficking to cybercrime, the communist dictatorship engages in a range of illegal activities to sustain its oppressive rule. Diplomats must recognize the detrimental consequences of this illicit trade, not only for the North Korean people but also for regional and global security. It is imperative that concerted efforts are made to dismantle these networks and hold those responsible accountable for their actions.

Strategies to Address Illicit Trade in Natural Resources in North Korea

Introduction:

Illicit trade in natural resources poses a significant challenge in North Korea, fueling the communist dictatorship and perpetuating its oppressive regime. This subchapter aims to unveil the strategies that can be employed to address this issue and curb the illegal trade of minerals, timber, and other natural resources. By implementing these strategies, diplomats can contribute to disrupting the shadow economy that sustains the North Korean regime.

1. Strengthen International Cooperation:

International collaboration and coordination are vital in combatting illicit trade in natural resources in North Korea. Diplomats can foster alliances with neighboring countries, regional organizations, and international bodies to share intelligence, enforce sanctions, and implement stringent measures against those involved in illegal activities. This cooperation can help identify smuggling routes, seize illicit shipments, and enhance information sharing to disrupt the illicit trade.

2. Enforce Trade Sanctions:

Diplomats should advocate for robust enforcement of trade sanctions targeting North Korea's natural resource trade. This includes restricting the export of minerals and timber, strengthening customs controls, and imposing penalties on individuals and entities involved in illicit trade. By pressuring states and corporations to comply with these sanctions, diplomats can limit the funds flowing into the communist dictatorship.

3. Enhance Monitoring and Surveillance:

To tackle illicit trade in natural resources, diplomats can support the adoption and implementation of advanced monitoring and surveillance technologies. This includes satellite imagery, unmanned aerial vehicles, and other high-tech solutions to detect and track illegal activities. By enhancing monitoring capabilities, authorities can identify smuggling hotspots, gather evidence, and facilitate more targeted enforcement actions.

4. Support Local Capacity Building:

Diplomats can play a crucial role in supporting capacity building efforts within North Korea. By providing technical assistance, training, and resources to local authorities, diplomats can help strengthen their ability to identify, investigate, and prosecute individuals involved in illicit trade. This can contribute to building a strong legal framework and fostering a culture of compliance within the country.

5. Raise Awareness and Promote Sustainable Alternatives:

Diplomats should engage in public diplomacy campaigns to raise awareness about the devastating impact of illicit trade in natural resources. By highlighting the environmental degradation, loss of biodiversity, and negative socio-economic consequences, diplomats can garner support for sustainable alternatives. This includes promoting responsible mining practices, sustainable forestry, and encouraging international investment in legitimate industries that can provide alternative sources of income for the population.

Conclusion:

Addressing illicit trade in natural resources in North Korea requires a multifaceted approach that combines international cooperation, enforcement of trade sanctions, enhanced monitoring, local capacity building, and promotion of sustainable alternatives. By implementing these strategies, diplomats can contribute to dismantling the shadow economy that sustains the communist dictatorship, fostering stability, and promoting a more prosperous future for the people of North Korea.

Chapter 13: Conclusion

Recap of North Korea's Illicit Businesses Supporting the Communist Dictatorship

Introduction:

In this subchapter, we will delve into the dark underbelly of North Korea's illicit economy, highlighting various illegal activities that support the communist dictatorship. By understanding these shadowy operations, diplomats can gain valuable insights into the regime's financial resources and potential vulnerabilities.

North Korea's Illegal Businesses to Support the Communist Dictatorship:

North Korea's authoritarian regime relies heavily on illicit businesses to sustain its grip on power. These activities include arms smuggling, counterfeit currency production, drug trafficking, human trafficking, cybercrime, nuclear proliferation, wildlife smuggling, money laundering, illegal fishing, and illicit trade in natural resources.

Arms smuggling: The illegal trade of weapons serves as a lifeline for the North Korean regime, providing funds and strengthening its military capabilities. Diplomats must closely monitor arms smuggling routes and actors involved to disrupt this dangerous trade.

Counterfeit currency production: The regime resorts to printing fake money to finance its operations and evade international sanctions. Understanding the counterfeiting techniques employed by North Korea is vital for diplomats to develop effective strategies to combat this illicit practice.

Drug trafficking: North Korea's involvement in smuggling and selling illegal drugs generates substantial income for the regime. Diplomats must collaborate with international law enforcement agencies to dismantle drug networks and prevent the flow of narcotics from North Korea.

Human trafficking: The illegal trade of humans for forced labor or exploitation is another abhorrent practice employed by the regime to finance its activities. Diplomats must work together to expose and disrupt these networks, protecting vulnerable individuals from exploitation.

Cybercrime: North Korea is notorious for its involvement in hacking, phishing, and other cyber activities for financial gain. Diplomats should focus on enhancing cybersecurity measures and collaborate with international partners to curb these cyber threats.

Nuclear proliferation: The illegal sale of nuclear materials or technology supports North Korea's nuclear program. Diplomats must remain vigilant in monitoring and countering proliferation networks to prevent the further advancement of North Korea's nuclear capabilities.

Wildlife smuggling: The illegal trade of endangered species and animal products generates profits for the regime. Diplomats should advocate for stronger international regulations and collaborate with conservation organizations to combat wildlife smuggling.

Money laundering: To make illicit funds appear legitimate, North Korea engages in various money laundering techniques. Diplomats must work closely with financial institutions, enforcing stringent anti-money laundering measures to disrupt the regime's financial networks.

Illegal fishing: North Korea engages in unregulated and illegal fishing activities to generate income. Diplomats must coordinate efforts to combat illegal fishing, protecting marine resources and depriving the regime of revenue.

Illicit trade in natural resources: Smuggling minerals, timber, or other natural resources is yet another avenue through which the regime generates income. Diplomats should advocate for stricter regulations and international cooperation to disrupt this illegal trade.

Conclusion:

Understanding the various illicit businesses supporting North Korea's communist dictatorship is crucial for diplomats. By comprehending these shadow economy activities, diplomats can effectively counter the regime's financial resources and work towards dismantling its oppressive regime. Through international collaboration and persistent efforts, the world can strive towards a future where North Korea's illicit businesses no longer sustain its communist dictatorship.

The Urgency for Action and International Cooperation

In today's interconnected world, the urgency for action and international cooperation to address the illicit activities supporting North Korea's communist dictatorship cannot be overstated. Diplomats from around the world must come together to tackle the various illegal businesses that enable this oppressive regime to maintain its grip on power.

One of the key aspects that demand immediate attention is North Korea's illegal businesses to support the communist dictatorship. These clandestine operations form the backbone of the regime's financial resources, allowing it to fund its oppressive policies and suppress its citizens. Addressing this issue requires a united front from the international community to cut off the revenue streams that sustain the regime.

Arms smuggling is one such illegal trade that must be combated. The North Korean regime engages in the illicit trade of weapons, supplying them to various actors that threaten regional and global security. International cooperation, including intelligence sharing and coordinated efforts to intercept these weapons, is crucial to disrupt their distribution networks and prevent further escalation of conflicts.

Counterfeit currency production poses another significant challenge. The regime prints fake money to fund its activities, including the oppression of its own people. This subversive practice undermines the global economy and demands a coordinated response from diplomats and financial institutions to identify and halt the circulation of counterfeit currency.

Drug trafficking is another illicit activity that warrants immediate attention. The regime smuggles and sells illegal drugs to generate income, contributing to the global drug trade and fueling addiction and crime. Diplomats must collaborate to dismantle the networks responsible for trafficking drugs and work towards rehabilitation and support programs for affected individuals.

Human trafficking, cybercrime, nuclear proliferation, wildlife smuggling, money laundering, illegal fishing, and illicit trade in natural resources are all interconnected issues that require international cooperation to combat effectively. By sharing intelligence, coordinating efforts, and imposing stricter regulations and penalties, diplomats can disrupt the financial lifelines that sustain the North Korean regime.

The urgency for action and international cooperation cannot be overstated. The atrocities committed by the communist dictatorship in North Korea necessitate a united front. Diplomats must work hand in hand to expose and dismantle the shadow economy that enables the regime's oppressive policies. Only through collaborative efforts can we hope to bring about a brighter future for the people of North Korea and ensure global peace and stability.

The Potential Impact on the Future of North Korea

As diplomats, it is crucial to understand the potential impact of North Korea's illicit businesses on the future of the country. The shadow economy supporting the communist dictatorship has far-reaching consequences that extend beyond its borders. This subchapter aims to shed light on the various illegal activities fueling the regime and the implications they hold for North Korea's future.

North Korea's illegal businesses to support the communist dictatorship have become a lifeline for the regime. Arms smuggling, for instance, not only allows North Korea to bolster its military capabilities but also contributes to regional instability. The proliferation of weapons can lead to conflicts and pose a threat to global peace.

Counterfeit currency production is another illicit activity that funds the communist dictatorship. By printing fake money, North Korea is able to maintain its grip on power and finance its extravagant lifestyle. However, this undermines the credibility of the international financial system and can lead to economic instability if left unchecked.

Drug trafficking is an alarming issue that not only generates income for the regime but also contributes to the global drug trade. The smuggling and sale of illegal drugs perpetuate addiction, fuel violence, and destabilize communities, both within North Korea and beyond its borders.

Human trafficking, a grave violation of human rights, is yet another illicit trade that finances the communist dictatorship. The illegal trade of humans for forced labor or exploitation not only perpetuates slavery-like conditions but also tarnishes North Korea's international reputation.

The rise of cybercrime poses a significant threat to global security. North Korea's involvement in hacking, phishing, and other cyber activities for financial gain not only undermines cybersecurity but also poses a threat to the stability of financial institutions and governments worldwide.

The illicit trade in nuclear materials or technology supports North Korea's nuclear program, which poses a grave danger to regional and global security. The illegal sale of these materials or technology can lead to the proliferation of nuclear weapons, heightening the risk of conflicts and nuclear terrorism.

Wildlife smuggling further exacerbates the environmental crisis and threatens biodiversity. The illegal trade of endangered species and animal products not only undermines conservation efforts but also fuels organized crime networks.

Money laundering is a crucial component of North Korea's illicit economy. By using illegal means to make illicit funds appear legitimate, the regime can continue to finance its activities while evading international scrutiny. This perpetuates corruption and hampers efforts to hold North Korea accountable.

Illicit fishing and the smuggling of natural resources also contribute to environmental degradation and economic exploitation. Engaging in unregulated and illegal fishing activities not only depletes fish stocks but also harms local communities that rely on these resources. Similarly, the smuggling of minerals, timber, or other natural resources undermines sustainable development and perpetuates economic inequality.

In conclusion, the illicit businesses supporting North Korea's communist dictatorship have severe implications for the country's future and global stability. As diplomats, it is crucial to address these issues collectively, enforcing stricter regulations, and holding the regime accountable. Only through concerted international efforts can we hope to curb the influence of these illicit activities and pave the way for a more prosperous and peaceful future for North Korea and the world at large.

www.ingramcontent.com/pod-product-compliance
Lightning Source LLC
Chambersburg PA
CBHW051250160726
47994CB00003B/1097